LeBron James

Revised Edition

By Jeff Savage

Lerner Publications ◆ Minneapolis

Lerner Publications Company
A division of Lerner Publishing Group, Inc.
241 First Avenue North
Minneapolis, MN 55401 USA

For reading levels and more information, look up this title at www.lernerbooks.com.

Library of Congress Cataloging-in-Publication Data

The Cataloging-in-Publication Data for *LeBron James* is on file at the Library of Congress.
ISBN 978-1-5124-0416-6 (pbk)
ISBN 978-1-5124-0417-3 (eb pdf)

Manufactured in the United States of America
1 – BP – 12/31/15

TABLE OF CONTENTS

Buzzer Beater	4
On the Move	10
Soaring High	13
Hitting the Big Time	17
Back Home	22
Selected Career Highlights	29
Glossary	30
Further Reading & Websites	31
Index	32

LeBron James *(right)* drives to the basket against Jimmy Butler of the Chicago Bulls.

BUZZER BEATER

LeBron James sprang into action at the beginning of the third quarter. He rose off the court for a **jump shot**. *Swish!* It was Game 4 of the second round of the NBA **playoffs** on May 10, 2015. The Cleveland Cavaliers were playing the Chicago Bulls at the United Center in Chicago. The Cavaliers had never won the NBA championship. But LeBron was back in Cleveland after playing in Miami for four seasons. Lots of people think LeBron is the best basketball player in the world. In 2015, Cavaliers fans were sure that he could help the team win a championship.

LeBron goes for a jump shot in the NBA playoffs.

LeBron and his wife, Savannah, have two sons, LeBron James Jr. and Bryce Maximus James. Their daughter, Zhuri James, was born October 22, 2014.

The game wasn't going well for Cleveland. At the end of the third quarter, the Cavaliers were behind the Bulls, 68–61. The Bulls played tough **defense** on LeBron and forced him to miss shots. He even twisted his ankle. But he wouldn't give up. "I was going to fight through it no matter what," he said.

LeBron faced tough defense from the Bulls.

With about seven minutes left in the game, the Cavaliers finally pulled ahead. J. R. Smith made a **three-point field goal** that gave Cleveland the lead, 71–70. Seconds later, LeBron knocked down two more points. But Cleveland couldn't stop Chicago superstar Derrick Rose from scoring. With just nine seconds left, Rose sank a shot to tie the game, 84–84.

Derrick Rose *(right)* goes up for a basket against the Cavaliers.

LeBron shoots the ball seconds before the buzzer rings.

The Cavaliers didn't have any **time-outs** left. But LeBron had a plan. "Give me the ball and get out of the way," he told his teammates.

LeBron took a long shot as the final seconds ticked away. The ball fell through the net just as the buzzer rang to mark the end of the game. The Cavaliers won, 86–84! LeBron ran to the center of the court to celebrate with his teammates. They were one step closer to their dream of winning the NBA championship.

The Cleveland Cavaliers celebrate their win.

LeBron grew up in Akron, Ohio.

ON THE MOVE

LeBron James was born December 30, 1984, in Akron, Ohio. He lived with his mother, Gloria. LeBron never met his father. "My mother is my everything," LeBron says.

Gloria and LeBron were very poor. They lived in a troubled part of town. At the age of five,

LeBron moved with his mother seven times. Once he lived in an apartment building that was so run-down the city had it closed and torn down. "I saw drugs, guns, killings," said LeBron. "It was crazy. But my mom kept food in my mouth and clothes on my back."

Gloria's boyfriend was a man named Eddie Jackson. LeBron called him Dad. Sometimes Jackson lived with LeBron and his mother. Other times, Jackson did not.

LeBron with his mom *(right)* and Eddie Jackson *(left)*.

LeBron's unsettled home life made school hard for him. He missed 82 days of school in fourth grade. So Gloria sent LeBron to live with his youth basketball coach, Frankie Walker. "It changed my life," said LeBron. In fifth grade, LeBron had perfect attendance and a B average. For the next few years, LeBron sometimes lived with Walker and other times with his mother.

LeBron loved playing sports. His favorite game was basketball. LeBron was a super player, even as a kid. In eighth grade, he led his school team to the finals of a national **tournament**. That same year, he threw down his first slam **dunk**. When he entered high school in 1999, LeBron was already more than six feet tall.

LeBron's amazing basketball skills made him one of the best high school players in the country.

SOARING HIGH

LeBron was a star at Saint Vincent-Saint Mary (SVSM) High School. As a freshman, he led the SVSM Irish to the Ohio state championship. He did it again in his sophomore year.

LeBron and his teammates celebrate winning the Ohio state championship during LeBron's freshman year.

That season, he was named Ohio's Mr. Basketball. This meant he was the top high school player in the state. He was the first sophomore to earn the title.

By his junior year, LeBron stood six feet seven inches tall. He was fast and very strong. He could jump incredibly high. Other high school players didn't stand a chance against him. Meanwhile, NBA **scouts** had been watching LeBron. "He's the best high school player I've ever seen," said one scout.

LeBron's skills made him famous. Thousands of people wanted to see him play. The SVSM gym didn't have enough seats to hold all the fans! So the Irish played its home games at the nearby University of Akron.

Tickets for LeBron's games sold for as high as $20. About 4,000 people showed up for each game. Even NBA superstars like Shaquille O'Neal came to see LeBron play. Los Angeles Lakers star Kobe Bryant gave LeBron a special pair of shoes with US flags on them.

Shaquille O'Neal *(above)* was one of several NBA players who came to see LeBron play at the University of Akron.

LeBron takes the ball to the hoop during his junior year in high school.

LeBron didn't let his fans down. In one game against the best team in the country, he scored an amazing 36 points. At the end of the season, scouts agreed that LeBron was already good enough to play in the NBA. They said that LeBron would be the first pick in the **draft** if he left high school a year early. "That is not going to happen," LeBron said. "I can do more to get my brain and my game ready if I finish school."

LeBron reads an article about himself in *Sports Illustrated* magazine. LeBron was famous around the country by his senior year in high school.

HITTING THE BIG TIME

LeBron was just 17 in 2002, when he started his senior year in high school. But it was hard for him to stay a kid. He was the most popular high school basketball player ever. He appeared on the cover of *Sports Illustrated* magazine. TV camera crews followed him to school every day.

But LeBron didn't let all the attention drive him crazy. He tried to live a normal life. He went to movies with his friends. He played games on his PlayStation 2. He ate huge bowls of Fruity Pebbles and Cinnamon Toast Crunch for breakfast—and dinner. He even made sure to keep his bedroom clean!

LeBron also worked on his game. He shot nearly 800 jump shots every day. Most important, he earned good grades. "He knows schoolwork comes first," said his mother. "No work, no basketball."

LeBron has a little fun while sitting at his locker.

LeBron's mom, Gloria, cheers her son on.

By LeBron's senior year, ESPN was showing his games on TV. In one game, LeBron scored 31 points and grabbed 13 **rebounds** to beat the top-ranked high school team in the country.

LeBron usually scored more than 30 points a game that year. Coach Dru Joyce said his star could have scored 50. But LeBron's favorite play has always been making a great pass. "I love sharing the ball with my teammates," he says. At the end of the season, LeBron's Irish were ranked first in the nation by *USA Today*.

LeBron shakes hands with NBA commissioner David Stern. LeBron was the first player taken in the 2003 NBA Draft.

Soon after, LeBron signed a **contract** with the Nike sports equipment company. He agreed to make ads for Nike for seven years. In return, they would pay him $90 million! LeBron was suddenly rich beyond his wildest dreams.

LeBron finished high school in the spring of 2003. In June, LeBron and his mom attended the 2003 NBA Draft. NBA **commissioner** David Stern walked onstage to announce the first pick: "With the first pick of the 2003 NBA Draft, the Cleveland Cavaliers select LeBron James."

LeBron walked up onstage in his fancy white suit. He smiled and shook hands with the commissioner. LeBron had become a pro. His dream had come true.

But the Cavaliers were a losing team. In 2002, they had the worst record in basketball. Cavaliers fans hoped LeBron could turn things around. But he was just 18 years old. Was he good enough to be a star in the best basketball league in the world? "There's a lot of pressure on me," he said, "but I don't put a lot of pressure on myself."

LeBron holds up his new Cleveland Cavaliers jersey. LeBron wore number 23 in honor of his favorite basketball player, Michael Jordan.

LeBron dribbles the ball during a game in 2004.

BACK HOME

LeBron made the Cavaliers a hot ticket for the 2003–2004 season. Fans across the country wanted to see the young **rookie** play. But was LeBron a good enough player to live up to the excitement? He soon showed that he was, scoring 21 points against the Phoenix Suns and 23 against the Indiana Pacers. But at the end of the season, the Cavaliers did not make the playoffs.

In the summer of 2004, LeBron played for Team USA at the **Summer Olympic Games** in Athens, Greece. The team finished in third place. Each player was awarded a **bronze medal**.

The next season, LeBron was named to play in his first **NBA All-Star Game**. He would go on to play in the All-Star Game in each of the next three seasons too. But Cleveland could not win the NBA championship. In 2008–2009, LeBron

LeBron goes up for a rebound against Phoenix Suns' player Shawn Marion at the 2005 NBA All-Star Game.

was named the NBA Most Valuable Player (MVP). The Cavs made it to the Eastern **Conference** Finals, but the team came up short again and lost to the Orlando Magic.

In the summer of 2008, LeBron returned to the Olympics, in Beijing, China. He and his teammates won the gold medal. "The US is back on top again," he said.

Cleveland had the NBA's best record in 2009–2010. LeBron was again voted to the All-Star Game and won the MVP award for the second year in a row. But once again, the Cavs failed to win the NBA championship.

Then, in the summer of 2010, LeBron announced on television that he was going to leave the Cavaliers. On a special show on ESPN called *The Decision*, LeBron said, "I'm going to take my talents to the Miami Heat."

Miami made it to the **NBA Finals** in 2011. But they lost to the Dallas Mavericks. The next year, Miami was back in the Finals again. This time, the Heat took the series against the Oklahoma City Thunder. LeBron had won his first NBA championship. "You know, my dream has become a reality, and it's the best feeling I ever had," he said.

LeBron looks for an opening during the 2012 NBA Finals. LeBron joined the Miami Heat in 2010.

LeBron makes a slam dunk during the 2012 Olympic Games.

LeBron wasn't done winning in 2012. That summer in London, England, he won his second Olympic gold medal. Then, in 2013, the Miami Heat won the NBA championship again.

After one more season in Miami, LeBron decided it was time to go home. On July 11, 2014, he announced that he was returning to the Cleveland Cavaliers. "I always believed that I'd return to Cleveland and finish my career there," he said.

On October 30, 2014, LeBron played his first game back in Cleveland. Huge pictures of the star **forward** hung outside the arena. Inside the arena, the crowd cheered loudly when he came onto the court. The whole city was excited that LeBron was home.

In 2015, fans voted LeBron to the NBA All-Star Game for the 11th time in a row. He went on to lead the Cavaliers to the 2015 NBA Finals. They faced Stephen Curry and the Golden State Warriors. LeBron scored 44 points in Game 1. This was the most he had ever scored in an NBA Finals game. He also had more points than any other player for the whole series. But Curry and the Warriors won the championship.

LeBron dribbles the ball during his first game back with the Cavaliers.

LeBron was disappointed. But winning basketball games isn't the most important part of his life. "I feel my calling here goes above basketball," he said. LeBron wants to help kids in his hometown of Akron. In 2010, he started the LeBron James Family Foundation with his mom. The foundation helps kids in Akron get a good education and stay healthy. "I think it's probably one of the best things I've ever been a part of," LeBron said. "It means so much."

The LeBron James Family Foundation encourages kids to stay healthy.

Selected Career Highlights

2014–2015	Played in his fifth NBA Finals in a row Voted to the NBA All-Star Game for the 11th time
2013–2014	Voted to the NBA All-Star Game for the 10th time Left Miami to join the Cleveland Cavaliers
2012–2013	Won the NBA Finals with the Miami Heat for the second year in a row Named NBA Finals Most Valuable Player for the second year in a row Named NBA Most Valuable Player for the second year in a row and fourth time overall Won his second gold medal as a member of the 2012 US Olympic basketball team
2011–2012	Won the NBA Finals with the Miami Heat Named NBA Finals Most Valuable Player Named NBA Most Valuable Player for the third time
2010–2011	Left Cleveland to join the Miami Heat
2009–2010	Named NBA Most Valuable Player for the second year in a row
2008–2009	Named NBA Most Valuable Player Won a gold medal as a member of the 2008 US Olympic basketball team
2007–2008	Ranked first in the league in scoring and third in total minutes played
2006–2007	Led all players in votes for the NBA All-Star Game
2005–2006	Named Most Valuable Player of the NBA All-Star Game
2004–2005	Won a bronze medal as a member of the 2004 US Olympic basketball team
2003–2004	Named NBA Rookie of the Year First player taken in the 2003 NBA Draft
2002–2003	Named Mr. Basketball in Ohio for the third time
2001–2002	Named Mr. Basketball in Ohio for the second time
2000–2001	First sophomore ever named Mr. Basketball in Ohio

Glossary

bronze medal: at the Olympics, a medal awarded to a third-place finisher

commissioner: the top official in the NBA

conference: one of two groups of teams in the NBA. The groups are the Western Conference and the Eastern Conference.

contract: a written deal agreed to and signed by a player and a team or a company

defense: actions that keep the other team from scoring

draft: a yearly event in which professional sports teams take turns choosing new players from a selected group

dunk: slamming the basketball through the hoop

forward: a player on a basketball team who usually plays close to the basket. Forwards need to rebound and shoot the basketball well.

jump shot: a shot made while jumping

NBA All-Star Game: a midseason game in which the best players in the league play

NBA Finals: the last round of the NBA playoffs. The team that wins the Finals becomes the NBA champions.

playoffs: a series of games to decide the league's champion

rebounds: grabbing missed shots

rookie: a first-year player

scouts: people hired by teams to look for future players

Summer Olympic Games: an event held every four years in which athletes from around the world compete in dozens of different sports

three-point field goal: a shot made from behind the three-point line on a basketball court

time-outs: pauses during basketball games when players rest and talk to their coaches

tournament: a set of games held to decide the best team

Further Reading & Websites

Fishman, Jon M. *Derrick Rose*. Minneapolis: Lerner Publications, 2015.

Fishman, Jon M. *Stephen Curry*. Minneapolis: Lerner Publications, 2016.

Savage, Jeff. *Super Basketball Infographics*. Minneapolis: Lerner Publications, 2015.

Cleveland Cavaliers website
http://www.nba.com/cavaliers
The official website of the Cavaliers includes team schedules, news, profiles of past and present players and coaches, and much more.

LeBron James: The Official Website
http://www.lebronjames.com
LeBron's official website features news, statistics, photos, and a blog from LeBron.

NBA website
http://www.nba.com
The NBA's official website provides fans with recent news stories, statistics, biographies of players and coaches, and information about games.

Sports Illustrated Kids
http://www.sikids.com
The *Sports Illustrated Kids* website covers all sports, including basketball.

Expand learning beyond the printed book. Download free, complementary educational resources for this book from our website, www.lerneresource.com.

Index

Akron, Ohio, 10, 15, 28

Chicago Bulls, 4, 6
Cleveland Cavaliers, 4–9, 20–24, 26–27
Curry, Stephen, 27

Dallas Mavericks, 25

Golden State Warriors, 27

Indiana Pacers, 22

James, Gloria, 10–12, 18–19, 28
Joyce, Dru, 19

LeBron James Family Foundation, 28

Miami Heat, 24–26

NBA Draft, 20

Oklahoma City Thunder, 25
Orlando Magic, 24

Phoenix Suns, 22

Rose, Derrick, 7

Saint Vincent-Saint Mary (SVSM) High School, 13, 15, 17, 19–20
Smith, J. R., 7
SVSM Irish, 13, 15, 19

Walker, Frankie, 12

Photo Acknowledgments

The images in this book are used with the permission of: AP Photo/Nam Y. Huh, pp. 4, 8, 9; David Banks/UPI/Newscom, pp. 5, 6; © Nuccio DiNuzzo/ Chicago Tribune/TNS via Getty Images, p. 7; © iStockphoto.com/Davel5957, p. 10; © Copyright. Akron Beacon. All rights reserved. Distributed by Valeo IP., pp. 11, 14, 17; © Bob Falcetti/Icon SMI, p. 13; © Jim Redman/Icon SMI, p. 15; © Michael J. Le Brecht II/NewSport/CORBIS, pp. 16, 18; AP Photo/Chuck Burton, p. 19; AP Photo/Ed Betz, p. 20; AP Photo/Tony Dejak, p. 21; © William Luther/San Antonio Express-News/ZUMA Press, p. 22; © John Gress/Icon SMI, p. 23; Mark Halmas/Icon SMI/Newscom, p. 25; © Timothy A. Clary/AFP/ Getty Images, p. 26; AP Photo/Tony Dejak, p. 27; AP Photo/Alex Menendez, p. 28; AP Photo/Ben Margot, p. 29.

Front cover: © Ezra Shaw/Getty Images.

Main body text set in Caecilia LT Std 55 Roman 16/28.
Typeface provided by Adobe Systems.